Recess

Recess

PRAYER MEDITATIONS
FOR
TEACHERS

ELSBETH CAMPBELL MURPHY

BAKER BOOK HOUSE
Grand Rapids, Michigan 49516

To Michael
and to the children and staff
of Albert Einstein Elementary School,
Hanover Park, Illinois

Contents

3. Prayers for the Grown-Ups

1

Prayers
for the Children

For the Child
Whose Brother I Taught

Lord, I have to talk about this kid—
He's not at all what I expected.
His brother was a shining star,
Superkid, perfected.

His older brother took home A's.
He drops his C's in puddles.
His brother was precise, intense.
This kid's a cheerful muddle.

His brother always raised his hand,
Followed instructions To The Letter . . .
What's that, Lord?

You know,
You're right!
I *do* like this kid better.

For the Latchkey Child

Father,
with what a mixture of anxiety and pride
he shows me the house key
tied firmly to his belt.
Other children are old hands
at going home to an empty house.
But this is his first day,
his first day of being alone and nervous,
of hearing funny noises.
"You'll be fine," I say.
"What rules did your mother give you?"
He has them all down pat.

Lock the door after me.
Phone Mom as soon as I get in.
Don't tell any callers I'm home alone.
Don't open the door to strangers.
Take the meat out of the freezer.
Set the table.
Do my homework.

The final bell rings.
"Well," he says grandly, shaking my hand,
"This is it."
I laugh and say,
"You'll be fine!"

Oh, Father, please let him be fine.
Guard him from fear and loneliness.
Oh, send an angel home with him.

For the Child Who Adores Me

Lord,
I'm writing this from the top of a pedestal.
Just why she placed me here,
I'll probably never know.
But here I am,
gulping the rarified air
and feeling a little rocky
as she gazes up at me,
unnervingly like a cocker spaniel.
Oh, dear.
I don't deserve this.
I mean, I *really don't deserve* this!
It's flattering, people tell me
in kindly amusement,
to have earned somehow
the admiration of a child.
But Lord, this kid likes me so much
she makes me nervous.
I'm afraid that someday
I'll inadvertently hurt her,
her love is so raw.
Oh, Lord,
I'm writing this from the top of a pedestal.
Show me a way
to step down gracefully
before I topple off.

For the Child Who Doesn't Like Me

I honestly don't understand it, Lord.
I don't know why she doesn't like me.

How do I know she doesn't?
Little things, I guess.
You know I don't take sass, Lord,
but she saunters along the edge.
She pushes as hard as she dares
against any rule she can.
She looks irritated when I praise her work—
as if, who am I to be saying these things?
And she doesn't—
well, it sounds kind of petty,
but she doesn't laugh at my jokes.
On purpose!

Little things, you know?
But they rattle me.
They rattle the precious image I hold
of myself
as some kind of pedagogical Pied Piper.
When you're a grown-up, a teacher,
and a kid doesn't like you.
it's downright embarrassing.

I try to be reasonable.
I think to myself, "It's simple.
We just have a personality clash."
But then I think,
"Where does she get off having a personality?
At least one that clashes with mine?"

So I don't know, Lord.
Where do we go from here?
If you could just somehow keep my chagrin
from sliding into anger and unfairness.
And if you could just somehow help her
learn,
in spite of her feelings for me.
And if you could just somehow—

Oh, Lord, I wish she'd come on over.

For the Chatterbox

Father,
one day, several years ago,
this child said his first word,
and so far the novelty hasn't worn off.
He's not a bad kid, Father.
He's not even all that noisy.
He's just so *incessant*—
chattering away to anyone and everyone
and on and on and on and on.
I've moved his seat so many times,
his desk should be on casters,
In desperation,
I banished him to the far corner of the room,
where he struck up a conversation
with the gerbils.

Father, I pray for peace and quiet.
No, not just for my sake,
but for his sake, too.
For there is a time to speak,
but there is also
a time to listen,
a time to reflect,
a time just to be
still.

So, Father, I don't ask that you take away
his gift of the gab.
But rather I ask
that you quiet him with your love
and let him receive, sometimes,
the gift of silence.

For the Restless Child

Lord,
this child
with her fidgets and wriggles
 and jiggles and joggles

(Just now
    she
       fell
          out
             of
                her
                   chair!)

is frazzling my
  jangling my
  jarring my
        NERVES!!!

Gentle Shepherd,
lead us both to calmer waters . . .

For the Child Who Fights

Father, this child glares at the world
through sullen eyes
and comes out swinging.
I'm not praying for understanding.
I understand him all too well.
He is every-man-for-himself.
He is look-out-for-number-one.
He is the-voice-of-anarchy-
in-a-world-gone-mad.
He is me.
(Or my baser instincts, anyway.)
Oh, Lord,
I *want* my classroom to be
a cradle of civilization.
I *want* to be a wise and gentle teacher
showing this child a Better Way.
But mostly I want to kill him.
He brings out the vigilante in my soul.
That's because it's hard to be wise and gentle
when I'm hauling someone out of line
for kicking.
For the fourth day in a row.
I have this fantasy
(and so far it's only that!)
of bouncing him against the wall
and screaming,
"When will you ever learn
that 'people are not for hitting?'
Take *that!*"
Splat!
No, Lord, I'm not praying for understanding.

I understand his angry spirit all too well.
I'm praying for . . .
Father, there's this other teacher I know of.
And, oh, what I wouldn't give
for even a little of his quiet strength,
his calm restraint!
He met this problem of violence, too,
and he could have wiped out the offenders.
With ten thousand angels.
But he didn't.

Lament

For John P.
Born—February 10, 1971
Died—December 20, 1978

Oh, Father, how the images come back to me!

At the Christmas party
he stood beneath the bright piñata,
blindfolded, swinging a plastic bat,
all energy and concentration,
intensely alive.

In less than an hour, he was dead.
Drowned. He fell through the ice
on his way home from school
for Christmas vacation.

On that first day back
I came in early to pack his things
and remove his desk
before the kids
could see it there,
so achingly empty, alone.

And the room was filled
with overwhelming sadness.
All silence—save for the voice of Rachel,
weeping for her children.

For the Child from Another Language and Culture

Lord, before I met her, I thought, "Oh, great!
I don't know how I'll deal with this—
to get a kid who's new to this country,
who speaks no English,
whose name I can't even pronounce.

How will I cope?"

But then
with what sweet courage she
walked into our babble.
And coped.

For the Child Whose Family Is Going Through a Divorce

Father, his family is going through a divorce,
and I'm supposed to watch him
for signs of strain.
Fighting with peers.
Crying at the slightest provocation.
Resisting authority.
Neglecting schoolwork.
Things like that.
His world is simply coming apart,
and I'm supposed to watch him
for signs of strain.

And what can I do to help him? I ask.
Offer him comfort and support, I'm told.
But how can he receive that from me?
Because to accept my help
would be to accept the awful truth.
He wants his family back together again.
No more.
No less.
And I, only his teacher,
wonder helplessly
when to clamp down
and when to ease up.
And in the meantime watch him
for signs of strain.

Oh, Lord, how can we ever say it—
that children are "resilient,"
"able to recover quickly
from illness, change, and misfortune"?
If they are at all,
it is only through a *miracle* of grace.
But forgive us, forgive us, forgive us
for speaking glibly,
for belittling their pain.
It's just that we adults are showing
signs of strain.

For the Child
Who Leaves
in the Middle of the Year

Father,
it's hard to describe her mood today.
Already she stands a little apart from us.
She's edgy, I guess,
and oddly subdued.
Eager to be off,
to start over,
to get the good-byes behind her,
yet so reluctant to let go and leave us.

We, too, are reluctant.
How hard it is
to think of someone we know
and like so much
being a stranger in a new place,
  entering a classroom that is not ours,
  sitting among classmates who are not
   these,
  greeting a teacher . . .

There's something unfinished
about this, Lord!
June . . . *June* . . . not January,
is the time for good-byes.
June—when they all leave together,
not January—with this one little piece of us,
broken off,
leaving alone.

She cleans out her desk
and turns in her books.
We have a party in her honor.
Her mother comes early
to pick her up.
I walk them to the classroom door.
A little too brightly I say,
"Remember your promise to write to us!"
She nods
and hugs me, quickly, tightly,
then turns and hurries away.

Aching, my heart calls after her,
"Go with God!"

For the Abused Child

Oh, God, hear me!
He says he got the bruises last night
when he fell down
in the bathtub
or was it the stairs
he says he doesn't remember which
but I know as surely as if I'd seen it all
that that's not what happened.
Oh, God. Oh, God.
Why is this happening?
They told us it might
they told us
to check.
I didn't really think it would ever happen
but even so
I accepted the mandate
because it was a mandate
and that's what we're supposed to do
so I put it on my list, you know,
so matter-of-factly
because I couldn't handle it any other way:
just the routine—
collect the lunch money
take attendance
lead the pledge
notice bruises . . .
Oh, God.
Let me think.
Okay. Get help.
I have to see the principal.
This kid, this . . .

I have to pray for him,
I have to pray,
but my thoughts lie heavy in my mind,
groaning like some poor wounded thing.
Oh, God.
This little boy.
Why am I so afraid?
And the principal stares at me,
mutely catching my alarm
behind the words,
"Um, could you come take a look
at one of my kids?
I think we might have a problem here."

For the Child Who's Going to Be Retained

Him: I flunked.

Me: No, you didn't "flunk." We talked about this before, remember? Your parents and I agreed that you need to repeat this grade.

Him: I flunked.

Me: Don't think of it like that. Think of it as getting a second chance. And if you work hard next time around, you'll catch up on all the stuff you didn't learn this year. *Then* you'll be ready to move on!

Him: I flunked.

Me: No, no, no. Please stop saying that.

But you know what, Father?
This kid flunked.
He's not being held back
because he's developmentally unready
or because he was ill
and missed a lot of school.
He's being held back
because he didn't do a lick of work all year.
He flunked.
And he needed to say that.
And I wouldn't let him.
In an effort to make him feel good
about himself,
I denied him the right
to feel bad about himself.

Oh, Father, it's a hard truth—
no adult can *make* a kid learn anything.
But when he said he flunked,
I told myself
I flunked.
So I wanted to rush him through
the valley of the shadow of failure
and out into the bright sunlight
of a new beginning.
Before he was ready.
I'm sorry.
He flunked.
He well and truly flunked.
And he has the courage to see it and name it.
And with courage like that,
maybe he'll turn his life around.
Wouldn't that be something?
Oh, wouldn't that be something?

For the Child
I Never Got to Know

It's become my end-of-the-year observance,
Lord, to place their composite picture
before me and look again at all those faces
as yet unformed, endearingly scruffy,
so alike, yet not the same.

I see again the kid so secretly dear
to my heart I wanted to smuggle him home
in my bag. And here's the kid who
so drove my mind to distraction I saw his
impish grin in ceiling cracks.
But here—

here I feel a sudden pang at the face
of the child I never got to know.
I ask myself how it can be that she remains
as much unknown to me now as then—
almost a stranger.

I wish attention were like cupcakes, Lord,
with exactly enough to go around—
no one getting too much or too little.
Oh, may she get extra attention next year!
Lord, I feel the loss of her! Does she
of me?

2

Prayers
for Special Times

At the Summer Workshop

For Bill Martin, Jr.

In July,
my group wrote poems on paper rainbows.
Another group played tambourines
and sang, with brimming hearts,
"The Grand Old Duke of York."
The leader beamed and called us by the name
Good Teachers.

In July,
September seems so far away.

Come September, there'll be seating charts
and worksheets, attendance books,
permission slips, referrals . . .
But, Father, let there always be

Tambourines! Poetry!

At the
Teacher's Supply Store

Father, help me.
It's the middle of August.
I'm standing outside
the teacher's supply store.
And I feel a spree coming on.
A smiling purple dinosaur (what else?)
calls to me from the window,
his speech balloon filled
by the two magic words:
"*Welcome Back!*"
Yes, it's that time again when teachers go
BACK TO SCHOOL!
And all of a sudden I'm
READY!
But that doesn't mean
I have to go crazy in there,
does it, Father?
I mean, do I really need:
    a rubber stamp smiley face that says,
      "Oops! Try again!"?
    a storytelling apron?
    a thirty-seven-inch birthdays calendar?
    a packet of origami paper?
    a packet of *any* flavor scratch-and-sniff
      stickers?
    a five-pound bag of plaster of Paris?
    a whole ditto master book on silent *e*?
Remind me, Father, of the value
of moderation.
Oh—and don't let me forget
to pick up one of those purple dinosaurs.

In My Classroom the Week Before School Starts

Awakened by the scrape
of my chalk, the room looks about
for the children.

After Waking Up
from a
School Nightmare

I lie in the darkness,
the fear receding,
the relief of wakefulness flooding in.
It was only a dream.
It was only a dream.

But, Father, it's always the same dream.
I'm late and I'm lost,
rushing through vaguely familiar corridors,
clutching desperately at my armload
of falling papers,
unable to find my own classroom.

Then suddenly
I'm there.
I throw open the door.
But it's too late.
The kids have gone wild.
And I can't stop them—
not with any
"classroom management" technique.
Everything has spun
hopelessly, wildly, totally
out of control.

Oh, Father, where does it come from—
this irrational terror of the night?

No matter.
In a few hours it will be morning.
All balance will be restored.
And I will be my rational self again—
a person who day after day
for hours on end
shuts herself alone in a room
with twenty-seven children.

Before the Class Comes Marching In

Well, Father, what do you think?
The room looks nice, doesn't it?
Breathe in. Breathe out. Relax. Relax.
Today is the first day of school.
And—depending on the class I get—
today *could* seem
like the first day of the rest of my life.
That's the funny thing about classes,
isn't it, Lord?
I mean, the *Class*
seems to have a personality all its own,
in addition to all the personalities in it.
The whole being greater
than the sum of its parts, and all that.
What do you think—
the room looks nice, doesn't it?
I've been thinking about it a lot, Lord,
and there are two messages
I want to get across right from the start:
    "Welcome, child!
    I believe in you!
    Together we can have
    a delightful year
    of learning and growth!"
And:
    "Nobody messes with me, kid!"
I think that just about covers it, Lord!
Breathe in. Br—
Oh! There's the bell.
Just one more thing, Lord.
You're not going anyplace, are you?

When My Class
Is the Greatest

Father, sometimes I call them to line up, and
trailing clouds of glory do they come
from the playground,
not quarreling,
but laughing and eager
to get back to work.
And sometimes I can't believe
how good they are.
And I think,
"This is it.
This is what it's all about.
And I can walk with kings,
because I am a *teacher*
and these are my sweet, beautiful students!"
But then I think,
"They've got to be up to something, right?"

On the Night of
Open House

"Hello!
Yes, please come in!"
Another Open House, Father,
and it doesn't get any easier,
awkwardly welcoming curious strangers
into my little room-world.
"Please feel free to look around."
I risked my life hanging those
paper bag owls
from the ceiling,
and they'd better notice them.
" 'How is she doing?'
Oh, fine—
but, actually, it's a little early in the year
to tell much . . ."
Help me, Lord!
Which one is theirs?
I don't have all the last names down yet.
"Jimmy!
How nice that your little brother
gets to see your room!"
Who let all these preschoolers in?
"But you must explain to him
that he can't go in the science corner
where we worked so hard
to set up our display!
How old is your little brother?"
Good! I have time to apply for a transfer.

"And you're Michael's parents?
Of course!
I certainly see a family resemblance!"
Yes, Lord, this explains a lot*!*
"What's that? Cindy
talks about me all the time?
Ha-ha. Nice things, I hope."
Good grief, Lord, what does she say?
"I'm so glad to have had this chance
to chat with you."
*Lord, please make Jason's parents
stop talking.
There's a line of other parents
waiting to meet me,
and I feel like a duchess
at a diplomatic reception.
Except that my feet hurt.
And I just want to go home
and watch TV.*
"Oh, yes, I agree with you.
It's always good to be able to put a face
with the name."
*Oh, Father, what do they think of me?
I'm a nice person—albeit a touch
ill at ease tonight.
And they're nice people—also ill at ease
as they peek into the world
I share with their children,
so apart from the world
they share with them at home.*

"I do appreciate your taking time
to come out tonight.
We're looking forward to a great year!"
And that's the truth.

On the Morning of the Standardized Test

MEMO TO: The Testmakers, Somewhere in Iowa or California
(I forget which)
FROM: A Teacher
RE: Your Standardized Test
DATE: Day of Administering Said Test

As you know, my school district spent *a lot* of money on your test, and therefore must take the results very, very seriously. This is a mistake. I'm writing to protest the unfairness of it all.

It is first and most importantly unfair to the children. There's something inside us all (the image of God, perhaps?) that objects to being scored and ranked. I recall one year the little boy who took one look at your test, burst into tears, and threw it on the floor. You gotta admire perception like that.

It's unfair to teachers, for we will be judged by a school district grasping at scores. Now, if you've ever seen a kid ... clutching a number 2 pencil ... trying to color in the tiny space between the dotted lines ... between the *right* dotted lines ... you'll appreciate why we're nervous.

It's unfair to the whole noble idea of Learning. Some districts, desperate for higher scores, have ordered teachers to teach the test. Only the test. Well, your test doesn't cover everything, and there are some things in life (perhaps most things of value) that can't be measured by a test at all.

It's time to get started. Your test manual instructs me to "Say: Good Morning," so I'd better go do that. I have just one more quick memo to write first.

MEMO TO: My Wise and Loving
            Heavenly Father

It's all so unfair, Lord. But I don't want to add to that unfairness. I want the kids at least to be able to give it their best shot. Help me, Father. Help me to do the best I can with something I don't believe in.

During the Fire Drill

The buzzer went off during math,
startling us so much
we couldn't for a moment
think what it was.
"Fire Drill," I said firmly.
"Line up quietly
in ABC order.
No talking.
No running.
No shoving or pushing.
Last one out,
turn off the lights
and close the door.
All set?
Let's go."

Oh, Father, is there anything more annoying
than a fire drill?
We couldn't stop for our coats, of course,
and it's too cold to be out here without them.
The kids are hopping up and down
and flapping their goose-pimply arms,
looking for all the world
like, well, goslings.
So cute and funny.
And suddenly,
so overwhelmingly
dear.
So vulnerable.

I guess that's what I hate about a fire drill:
It makes me think,
What if?
What if there were a real fire?
Could I get the kids out safely?
Would our wing
(as per the instruction leaflet)
exit quickly and calmly
by the northwest door?
I hate hearing about disasters—
about fires and floods and earthquakes
and tornadoes,
the sound of the whole creation groaning,
reminding us that we live in a fallen world.

But worst of all
are the evils we make for ourselves.
Oh, Father,
from hunger
and violence
and war
and poverty
and illiteracy
and injustice
give us the grace to protect our children,
all the children of the world.

"Hey! The other classes are going in now!"
The children stare at me
in uneasy bewilderment
as I swallow hard
and fumble for a kleenex.
"All right, let's go,"
I say more gruffly than I mean to.
"No running.
No pushing or shoving.
Someone could get hurt."

Sunday Night Insomnia

Oh, Father,
how is it possible
to be so wearied and so wired
all at the same time?
The luminous numbers glare at me
as if to say,
"Aren't you sleeping *yet*?!
How do you expect to get up for school
in the morning??"
Yet that's what's keeping me awake—
having to get "up" for school.

How much easier Monday morning would be
if I could just shuffle over to my desk
with a cup of coffee and a donut,
write out my to-do list in peace,
piddle about with some papers,
ease myself into the week.
How much simpler teaching would be
if the kids didn't arrive
until sometime around Tuesday afternoon.

But Monday morning they are there—
bright-eyed and bushy-tailed,
spilling book club money out of their mittens,
chattering away to me
in dialogue straight from
theatre of the absurd:
"You know what?
Yesterday we went by my grandma's?
But one of the fish was dead!"

Oh, Father,
I need some sleep.
I'm a teacher.
I don't have the luxury
of a sluggish Monday morning.
If anything,
I have to be brighter and bushier than they.
I am, after all, Head Squirrel.
At what point did I stop making sense?
Maybe this means I'm drifting off.
Father,
I have to get up for school tomorrow.
And I need your gifts
of strength
and peace.
And sleep.
I need some sleep . . .

On the Night
of the Big Program

Oh, they're all decked out
  In their antlers and bells—
Supposed to be reindeer.
  (Can anyone tell?)

Their spirits are high;
  They're full of good cheer.
(Which is trying the patience
  Of some of us here.)

"Okay, everybody, line up—
  And don't crowd.
Don't fall off the bleachers;
  Just sing nice and loud."

(That tune, learned in Music
  In time for tonight,
Will ring in my brain
  For the rest of my life.)

"And then, when your part of the concert
  Is done,
We'll wait in our classroom."
  (Won't *that* be fun.)

Lord, they're all so excited
  At being out late,
At having the spotlight . . .

"Wow! You guys did GREAT!"

When the Whole Class Flunks the Test

Father,
I'm sorry I yelled at them like that,
I really am.
It's just . . . I mean . . .
how could this *happen*?
Sure, I expected a few would mess up,
but *all* of them?
I honestly thought they were getting it!
What were we doing all that time?
All my creative song-and-dance,
all my review and hard-nosed drill,
how could it come to . . . to nothing?
HOW CAN THEY NOT KNOW
THIS STUFF??

Father,
I'm not sure I even want
what I'm about to ask for,
but here goes:
Insight (to know what went wrong)
Wisdom (to find a better way)
Patience (to—oh, help us!—try again)
Perspective (it isn't, I guess,
the end of the world)
Oh, and toss in a little humor, too, okay?
(I could sure use some!)

When It Might Be a "Snow Day"

Wow, it's really come down out there, Lord!
But when is too much snow
enough snow
to close the schools?
I can't imagine
they're going to have school today . . .
But it's 6:17,
and Peggy hasn't called me yet.
The superintendent calls the principal,
the principal calls Peggy,
Peggy calls me,
I call Marilyn and Gary . . .
It's really coming down!

Oh, Lord, I need a white day—
a day not scribbled up with lesson plans,
a day unmeasured by nerve-jarring bells—
a downy comforter of a day
a marshmallow day
a snow day.

On such a day
I might bake bread.
I might read a novel.
I might bake bread *and* read a novel.

But such a day cannot be taken
when school's going on without me,
and I'm not *really* sick enough to be home.
No, such a day
can only be given.
Oh, Lord, I need a snow day.

It's 6:38.
The telephone's ringing.
Oh, please, let it be Peggy.
Oh, please, please, please, please, please!

When I Get Flak

*Deliver me from my enemies, O God.**
   Enemies!
   What am I doing with enemies?
   What is the matter with these people?
   This is the first I knew
   anything was wrong!

Protect me from those who rise up against me.
   It seems one of them
   didn't like
   the way I graded some papers.
   (Or something like that.
   I'm not sure I follow it all.)
   So she phoned all the other parents
   and led a stormy little group of them
   straight to the principal's office.

I have done no wrong,
   Lord, you know I don't deserve this!
   From a molehill of a misunderstanding
   she has churned up a mountain of spite.

yet they are ready to attack me.
   Why?
   Why are they ready to attack me?
   I work so hard!
   I care so much!
   Is this how they pay me back
   for all the love I've given their kids?

*Selected verses from Psalm 59 (NIV), a psalm of David when Saul had sent men to watch David's house in order to kill him.

Arise to help me; look on my plight!
> My plight
> is that I'm hurt and bewildered.
> (How could they do this to me?)
> Unsure of myself.
> (Do I really know what I'm doing?)
> Lonely.
> (Other teachers get this, too, right?
> Right?)
> And so mad I feel sick.

O my Strength, I watch for you;
you, O God, are my fortress, my loving God.
In the morning I will sing of your love;

> because I think today
> is pretty much shot.

When a Child Comes Back to Visit After Many Years

We sat at lunch around the table, Lord,
when another teacher, beaming,
came in and exclaimed, "What a boost!"

He was having a bad day
in a bad year with a rough bunch of kids
and little to show for all his time and work.

He'd been spending a frenzied lunch time
alone in his room
where the principal found him
and smiling said, "You have a visitor
waiting for you in the office; come on!"

The teacher, wondering, hurried there and saw
a gangly, awkward, eager teen-aged boy.
And flashing back eight years, he saw
and exclaimed, "Tony!"

The mother laughed with pleasure.
"Wow! I'm impressed!
Do you remember all of them like that?"
"Oh," said the teacher, "I couldn't forget—
not Tony!" But I might have, he thought,
the way I blank out on names.
By what grace did it come, was sent,
to my lips just now? "Tony!"

Eight years ago in the life of a child is forever.
Eight years ago
and a thousand miles to this meeting.

The mother laughed again and said, "You're all
he's talked about for months—
ever since we planned to come back home to visit.
'Will he still be there?' he asked,
'I have to go and see. Will he remember me?
Will he?' " The teacher remembered
a bright but struggling little boy for whom
the weight of the world was packed
in just two words: First Grade.

By what grace, the teacher wondered,
did I sense to kneel beside him long ago,
to rub his back and whisper
that it would be all right?
What angel restrained my anger at his tears?

Now Tony, tongue-tied, stood before his friend
and smiled that well-remembered,
winsome smile.
His mother said, "You see he's shy, still shy."
The teacher said, "I, too, am shy.
It's okay to be shy."
And shyly then they all shook hands.

The boy had asked a thousand times,
"Will he still be there?"
And the teacher thought, I was here!
I was here!

We sat at lunch around the table, Lord,
and thought about how much we influence
these lives.
Exultant thought!
Yet frightening, too.
Lord, help us not to be afraid,
but trusting, teach them by your grace.

When My Class Is the Pits

Remind me, Lord, this, too, shall pass.
This class
shall pass.

3

Prayers
for the Grown-Ups

When I'm the Teacher—
Everywhere

Lord,
when the maitre d' asked,
"How many in your party?"
I answered, "FOUR!"
and held up four fingers.

But that's not all.

My answering machine
instructs the caller
to sit up straight
and speak directly into the phone.

I circle the spelling mistakes
on supermarket flyers.

I switch off TV talk shows
when the speakers won't take turns
and raise their hands.

I just . . . I just . . .
want all the people in the whole world
to stay in their seats
and put their names on their papers.

Lord, help me.

For the First-Year Teacher

The first-year teacher
looks a little lost, Father—
as if they might have forgotten
to tell her a few things
in teacher training.
They certainly forgot with me!
But I've picked up a bit of know-how
over the years,
and I'd like to pass along
what I've learned.

Dear First-Year Teacher,

Your training is not over; it's just beginning. A good teacher must first and always be a learner. And you learn to teach by teaching. There is no other way.

So you must come to your first job now with both humility and confidence—humility because you don't know it all, and confidence because you know more than you think you do.

As you've no doubt painfully discovered, teachers are not as valued and respected by our society as they should be. Well, the way to begin changing that is to first of all respect yourself and your work. Your work is of immeasurable and lasting importance. (How many people can say that?) And you have the heart and soul of a teacher. You're a professional. So begin, without being rigid, to develop a point of view, a personal philosophy of education. Then trust your instincts. Who knows better about what succeeds in your classroom than you?

A word about personality: As a teacher, you really need to have one. In fact, a touch of megalomania doesn't hurt. You need to come into the classroom each day with the attitude that "I'm the Teacher, and I'm in charge here." You don't have to be nasty about it, of course, but your presence has to be felt. After all, if *you're* not in charge of your room, who is?

A further word about personality: The one you have should be your very own, not someone else's. This means that you must organize your classroom in a way that fits you. For example, if you are quiet and serious, don't feel that you must suddenly become perky, just because you signed a contract. Kids require two things of their teachers—niceness and fairness. Beyond that, they're more than willing to adapt to who you are. You can return the favor. Learn the age-level characteristics of the grade. And study the developmental stages above and below, too. That way you'll know where your kids are coming from and where they're going. General characteristics can carry you only so far, of course; get to know the *people* in your class. It's an old maxim, but it bears repeating: You're not just teaching a class, you're teaching individuals in that class.

So get to know your kids and let your kids get to know you. Be yourself. And bring your enthusiasms into the classroom. Are you crazy about underwater photography and Abyssinian cats? Share that with your kids! They'll love you for it. And they'll start sharing of themselves, too.

Having covered Personality, we come now to the Pencil Sharpener. Why do they never tell you in teacher training how important the pencil sharpener is? I mean by this, of course, that you have to decide how you're going to handle Every Picky Little Thing. Can the children get up to sharpen a pencil any time they want to? Or are you going to have them line up by rows at specified times? It's up to you, of course, but the point is, you have to *think* about it; it won't just take care of itself. The details of classroom management can drive you crazy. But if your "Rules for Our Room" doesn't look like the Manhattan Yellow Pages, you probably haven't covered everything.

Don't be dismayed if you find yourself saying no a lot more than you'd like to. It's all because you have this *group*. Sure, you'd like to tell the individual kid he can stretch his legs and get a drink of water, but if you do, you could be killed in the stampede.

Speaking of the group, it's very important to accept the class you get. This doesn't mean that you won't work with them or push them to do and be their best. But it does mean that thou shalt not covet thy neighbor's class because she has higher reading groups and fewer behavior problems. Your kids are *your* kids.

Never let yourself slip into a Them-against-Me mentality. While a classroom may be more like a benevolent dictatorship than a democracy, you *are* all in this learning-thing together. Don't start thinking that the kids are out to get you. They're not.

Having said that . . .

You will from time to time have *absolutely rotten* days. And if a nonteaching friend says in bewilderment, "They're just little kids; how bad can they be?" don't even try to explain.

Naturally, some of your best friends will be teachers, because you all understand what the world of school is like. But important as it may be to talk through your teaching experiences, be careful not to rehash your days. Talk about something else sometimes!

It's easy to feel as a teacher, especially in your first year, that your job has swallowed you alive.

Let me explain why you're feeling overwhelmed. It's because you're overwhelmed. It's a best-kept secret, but let's bring it out in the open. There's no way in the world you can cover everything the state or local school district tells you that you have to cover. And it seems to be getting worse instead of better. How many times have you heard someone with a cause (maybe a perfectly good cause) say, "We've got to address this in our *schools*"?

So it all adds up to more hours than there are. This means that you have to set realistic goals and priorities. You can't do this all on your own. You have to get a feel from the principal and the other teachers as to what's most important, where to concentrate your time and effort.

Tune in to what the other teachers are doing around you, but be careful not to compare yourself too much with others. A topflight teacher can make you feel inadequate; a lousy teacher can make you feel smug. It's not just a matter of how many hours a teacher puts in, so don't set undue store by that. In every school there's someone who stays till six o'clock every night, and there's someone else who adamantly leaves at three o'clock carrying home nothing but her purse. Neither extreme is realistic, and somehow (through trial and error, I guess) you have to find what works for you.

Speaking of what works, we should say a word about curriculum. A healthy skepticism is in order. I once had a textbook manual tell me that while I was working with a small math group at the front of the room, another small group could be at the back of the room, unsupervised, building a table. Nope.

Make careful lesson plans, but be prepared to "go with the flow."

That's because everything takes longer than it should. (If you allow fifteen minutes to carve the jack-o-lantern, it will take fifteen minutes just to spread out the newspapers.)

That's because nothing takes up as much time as it should. (If you pass out ditto puzzles to fill a dragging afternoon, two minutes later the kids will all be waving the thing in the air, yelling, "FIN-ISHED!")

You have to go with the flow because each teaching day is an experience unto itself, full of surprises. A bat in the multipurpose room, for example, is an interruption to be reckoned with. So you might as well do a miniscience lesson on bats.

But most of all, you have to go with the flow because your kids need you to attend to them. They might have something on their minds— any little thing from the "misty, moisty morning" to a snapshot of someone's new puppy. And it makes them restless until they've had a chance to be heard and have received an acknowledgment from you. So listen to your kids. And pay attention to the small stuff of life.

Teaching. Surely one of the toughest and most rewarding jobs in the world! What am I forgetting? Oh, yes. Don't skip lunch.

> Well, Father,
> that's what I've picked up
> over the years.
> I don't know if it will be
> of any help to her.
> But I *do* know this:
> The most important help
> any teacher can have
> is a sense of your presence
> in the everydayness
> of classroom life.
> The first-year teacher
> looks a little lost, Father.
> Watch over her.

For the Principal

For Marv

You hear a lot of horror stories, Father,
and I know firsthand
that at least some of them
are true.

There was the principal who
kept her hot, tired teachers late
at an after-school meeting
while she read them a poem
of her own composing.
Twenty-six stanzas.
One for each letter of the alphabet.
On dental health.

There was the principal who
banished library books
from the classrooms
and forbade his teachers
to read to their children—
because he thought it interfered
with the basal scope-and-sequence chart.

There was the principal who . . .
but never mind.
This kind of talk
can pull me down pretty fast.

I will think instead of my current principal.
He is worth far more than rubies.

But not for a whole multipurpose room
full of rubies
would I want his job.
It's sort of like being
a pastor
or a president.
Everyone—*everyone*—
has an opinion about you.
And they're more than willing
to share it.
Stubborn superintendents.
Angry parents.
Frustrated teachers.
Life is a round of meetings
and paperwork,
and to top it all off,
misbehaving kids.

Yet he does the job with humor and kindness
when it's a wonder anyone
can do it at all.

We don't pray for them enough,
do we, Father?
The principals, I mean.

Dear Lord,
Preserve the good ones.
Improve (or remove!) the bad ones.
And let us all work together in harmony.
For the sake of our schools,
our kids.
Amen.

For the Librarian

Her title is:
Multimedia Learning Center Specialist.
But she has this thing about *books* . . .
So one day she rose up
and announced with crusty pride,
"I am a *li-brar-ian*!
And this—
this is a *library*!"
Then all the people said,
"Amen!"
So we made a new sign for her door.
And on the shelves,
the books were
grinning from cover to cover.

For the Consultants

Father,
I'm afraid there's a lot of friction here.
That's because
when you're a classroom teacher,
the world is divided
into two groups of people:
those who have to make a bunch of kids
shut up and sit down
and those who don't.
Consultants don't.
And furthermore,
they can go to the bathroom
anytime they want.
Most consultants, it's true,
used to be classroom teachers.
But the opinion from the trenches
is that they no longer wear the Green Beret.
Still,
it's not easy being a consultant,
working within a slow and clumsy system
where a child referred today
is lucky to get placed next year.
Father,
I'm afraid there's a lot of friction here.
We all need to be anointed
with the oil of your peace.

For the Team

Father, I'm afraid I often take these people for granted, but we wouldn't be able to have school without them. Lord, I want to thank you for the team.

Here is a person who greets all visitors to the school; who orients substitute teachers; who knows what callers want even when they're not sure themselves; who can understand what kindergartners are saying; who can read the most scribbled, cryptic notes from teachers; who watches over kids who are either too sick or too bad to go out for recess; who holds the place together and brings new meaning to the term *organized*. Lord, I want to thank you for the secretary!

When children get sick, they get scared. Even a mild stomachache can seem like appendicitis to them. They need someone who responds with capable serenity, offers matter-of-fact sympathy. They also need someone who can spot a phony from clear down at the end of the hall. Lord, I want to thank you for the nurse!

Without going into details, sometimes something happens in my room that causes me to run gagging into the hall. That's when he calmly takes over. There are days when his job is not unlike that of a zoo keeper in all its yuckiness. And even on the pleasantest days, classrooms need upkeep and repair. Lord, I want to thank you for the custodian!

Some people think kids are always bubbling over with eager questions about the universe. Not really; but there *is* one question that gets asked a lot: What's for lunch? For all their interest in food, it's heartbreaking to see the perfectly good food they throw away. It's even more distressing to watch them eat. A school cafeteria is not the pleasantest place in the world— most factories are quieter—but there are people who cheerfully care for school children in this special way. Lord, I want to thank you for the cafeteria workers!

Children are not the most alert of all your creatures. If somebody didn't stop them, they'd walk right out into the traffic. Somebody stops them. Lord, I want to thank you for the crossing guard!

Here is a person with nerves of steel, who takes on the awesome responsibility of getting a bunch of wired kids from there to here and back again. I can't imagine doing it. Lord, I want to thank you for the bus driver!

No, we couldn't have school without them. Lord, I want to thank you for the team!

Schooldaze

Oh, Lord . . .

These tedious quarrels!
This petty pride!
Childish jealousies!
Choosing sides!
Not to mention
the snotty clique
going off
in a fit of pique!
School is wearisome at best.
(I had to get that off my chest.)
I came to you,
I'm glad I did,
but now let's talk
about the kids.

For the Parents of a Gifted Child

Father, truly it must be unnerving
to have a child that smart,
to gaze on one's own offspring,
as they do,
with tickled awe.
We've met to decide what's best for him.
We, who don't know what to make of him.
Omniscient God,
what shall we do for this child?
Enrichment programs?
Private lessons?
Skipped grades?
Special classes?
His parents wonder what to give this boy
to whom so much has already been given.
But maybe there is still one thing.
And maybe it's something only they can give.
And maybe it's the smartest gift of all—
childhood.

For the Parents
of a Struggling Child

Father,
they come to the parent-teacher conference
warily,
wearily,
knowing full well
what they're not going to hear.
They won't hear
that their son is in the top reading group,
or that he's a whiz at math,
or that his penmanship is flawless,
or that he's entering the science fair,
or that he was last to sit down
at the spelling bee.

But, Father,
let them hear what I have to say.

Let them hear
that even though school is hard for him
(and probably always will be),
he never gives up.
He struggles on until he gets it,
and what he's learned, he's *earned*;
it's his to keep.

Let them hear
that this report card doesn't mean
their son's not good enough.
Rather, this standard of measurement
isn't good enough to measure him.

Father,
let me say
and let them hear
that he's as fine and brave and good a person
as ever I've met.

They came this evening
warily,
wearily.
Let them go home satisfied
and proud.

For the Parent of a Coddled Child

He lifts her over the snowdrifts
when maybe the thing to do
is bundle her up,
wish her well,
and let her plow on through.

For the Troubled Parents

How shall I put it, Lord?
On the great worksheet of life,
these people don't color inside the lines.
They are,
in the parlance of the teachers' lounge,
the wacko parents,
the lunatic fringe,
who can make a teacher's life miserable.
So we laugh to help ourselves feel better.
But it's an uneasy laugh at best.
Because these are troubled people,
and their kids are growing up
in troubled homes.
We know we can't make the problem go away.
So we laugh.
Who can help them, Lord, but you?
Grant me the grace,
when I'm tempted to hold them in derision,
to hold them out to you
in prayer.

In Praise of Parents

There are people who faithfully save paper-towel rolls and cottage cheese containers (even when they hate cottage cheese) just because you've said you need them for "a project," and these same people never laugh at you or ask you why.

There are people who don a costume and march around the neighborhood in the Halloween parade, even though there's a good chance they'll run into somebody from the bank.

There are people who get plaques made of spray-painted macaroni shells for Christmas and who actually hang them on the wall for everyone to see.

There are people who stay up half the night arranging tiny red candy hearts into smiley faces on Valentine cupcakes.

There are people who hold bake sales and fun fairs and something called "pizza day" to raise money for a learning center computer.

There are people who take time off work to come to school for something called "career day," where they try to explain to a bunch of puzzled kids (their own included) what in the world they do for a living.

There are people who voluntarily climb on a bumpy school bus, where the decibel level can't even be measured, and ride 7,000 miles to the zoo. Then these same people—all in the name of education—accompany their little group into the ape house amid cries of "Eeewwwww! It stinks in here! That one looks just like my brother! Eeewwwww! Do you see what he *did*?"

There are people who help with homework, sign report cards, run dittos, who show up for the school play and applaud until their hands ache.

And then these same people tell you that you're doing a great job and that their kids love school because of you.

There are people called parents.

Thanks, Lord!

For the Teacher Who's Going into Real Estate

Peggy turned in her letter of resignation
first thing this morning, Lord.
She won't be back, come fall.
And because rumor travels
at the speed of light
around this place,
everyone knew about it
before the second bell.

By some uncanny coincidence,
several of us led our bewildered classes
out to an extra-early recess
all at the same time.
Then, saying to our little hangers-on,
"GO PLAY!"
we settled down to the business at hand.

How could she do it? one of us demanded of
Peggy. Such a good teacher! How could she
abandon the kids and the Cause of Education
in America? But someone else interrupted to
ask if Peggy's office had any more openings.
And someone else advised her to keep her cer-
tificate current so that she could always come
back. Then someone else wondered aloud if it
could be burnout—and how do you know when
you've had enough? And all of us agreed that

teaching is the hardest job there is and that it's harder than it has to be. And why couldn't there be more clerical help and smaller classes and more money and more . . . more *respect*?

And so it is
that Peggy's leaving teaching, Lord,
and going into real estate.
She won't be back, come fall.

At the School Board Meeting

Lord,
let me feel you near me!
It's so hard to concentrate
in this burring, overheated room.
I'm here to represent my school.
And soon it will be my turn
to step out from the crowd
and address my well-reasoned plea
for smaller class sizes
to the school board.
They're sitting on the dais,
behind that staunch, impassive table,
and I have the strangest idea
that I won't be nearly big enough
to reach the microphone,
that my small voice will be swallowed
in the mechanical shrilling.
Nervously, I gulp the bitter, tepid coffee
and wait my turn to speak.

And suddenly I'm thinking
of the oddest things:

> the crisp, satisfying sound of scissors cutting
> into good construction paper;
> the yucky smell of lima beans wrapped in damp
> paper towels to germinate;
> the warm, trembly feel of the gerbil when I
> gently lift him out of his cage to say hello to
> everyone;

the bright, orderly beauty of Cuisenaire rods
in the midmorning sunlight;
the happy taste of popcorn on our Friday after-
noons when soon it's going-home time and
all's right with the world.

"Hey, you're on!"
The local newspaper reporter,
who covers education,
nudges me
and nods toward the microphone.
My turn.
My turn to somehow
make all these grown-ups see
that when class sizes are too large,
children have to wait too long
for their turn to hold the gerbil.
Lord, let me feel you near me!
I am a stranger far from home.

In Praise of a Teacher

For Mr. Porter

One of our best teachers is retiring, Lord, and we've all been asked to offer a brief tribute. I want to say something glowing, something worthy of him, and the statement that comes to mind is this: He showed up.

That doesn't sound like much, I know. But I am reminded of a little girl I once knew who came home discouraged from her first day at kindergarten. When her mother asked her what she had learned that day, she sighed and said, "Not much. I have to go back tomorrow."

How often we say that children grow up so fast, but that's not true. Growing up is a long, slow process, and kids need people who will show up for them, to teach and nurture them — tomorrow after tomorrow after tomorrow.

Not everyone is willing or able to do that — to put so much into a job that offers so little in the way of money or perks or prestige. So why did he do it? For over forty years? Because he had this crazy, unshakable idea that kids are more important than anything else in the world. So he was a teacher, and he showed up.